KU-495-724

# What's Living in Your Kitchen?

Andrew Solway

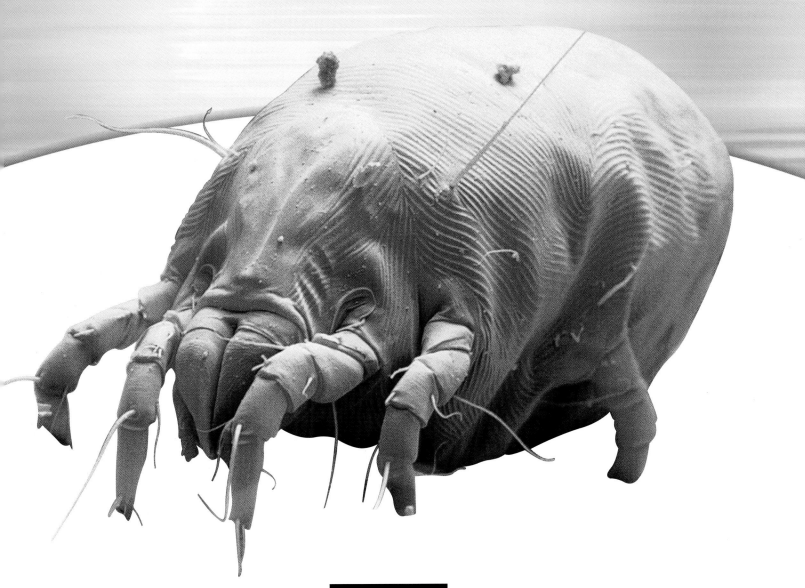

Heinemann
LIBRARY

**www.heinemann.co.uk/library**
Visit our website to find out more information about **Heinemann Library** books.

To order:
 Phone 44 (0) 1865 888066
 Send a fax to 44 (0) 1865 314091
Visit the Heinemann Bookshop at www.heinemann.co.uk/library to browse our catalogue and order online.

First published in Great Britain by Heinemann Library, Halley Court, Jordan Hill, Oxford OX2 8EJ, part of Harcourt Education.
Heinemann is a registered trademark of Harcourt Education Ltd.

© Harcourt Education Ltd 2004
The moral right of the proprietor has been asserted.

All rights reserved. No part of this publication may be reproduced, stored in a retrieval system, or transmitted in any form or by any means, electronic, mechanical, photocopying, recording, or otherwise, without either the prior written permission of the publishers or a licence permitting restricted copying in the United Kingdom issued by the Copyright Licensing Agency Ltd, 90 Tottenham Court Road, London W1T 4LP (www.cla.co.uk).

Editorial: Nancy Dickmann and Tanvi Rai
Design: David Poole and Paul Myerscough
Illustrations: Geoff Ward
Picture Research: Rebecca Sodergren
Production: Séverine Ribierre

Originated by Dot Gradations
Printed and bound in China by South China Printing Company

The paper used to print this book comes from sustainable resources.

ISBN 0 431 189633
09 08 07 06 05
10 9 8 7 6 5 4 3 2

**British Library Cataloguing in Publication Data**
Solway, Andrew
Hidden Life: What's Living in Your Kitchen?
 579.1'7554
A full catalogue record for this book is available from the British Library.

**Acknowledgements**
The publishers would like to thank the following for permission to reproduce photographs:

Alamy Images p. **6t**; Corbis pp. **4t**, **19** (RF), p. **13t** (Jacqui Hurst), p. **22r** (Sally A Morgan); Holt Studio International p. **8**; Science Photo Library p. **20** (CAMR, Barry Dowsett), p. **17** (Martin Chillmaid), pp. **7**, **27**, **23**, **25** (Eye of Science), p. **21** (DrGary Gaugler), p. **24b** (Eric Grave), p. **5** (R. Maisonneuve, Publiphoto Diffusion), p. **6b** (Medical Stock Photo), p. **9** (Susumu Nishinaga), p. **14** (Noble Proctor), pp. **10**, **13b** (Rosenfeld Images Ltd), p. **16** (Prof. N. Russell), pp. **4b**, **10t**, **10b**, **15** (David Scharf), p. **12** (Scimat), pp. **26**, **27b** (Sinclair Stammers), p. **22L**, **24T** (Volker Steger); Tudor Photography p. **18**.

Cover photograph of a meal mite, reproduced with permission of Science Photo Library/Science Pictures.

Every effort has been made to contact copyright holders of any material reproduced in this book. Any omissions will be rectified in subsequent printings if notice is given to the publishers.

**Disclaimer**
All the Internet addresses (URLs) given in this book were valid at the time of going to press. However, due to the dynamic nature of the Internet, some addresses may have changed, or sites may have ceased to exist since publication. While the author and publishers regret any inconvenience this may cause readers, no responsibility for any such changes can be accepted by either author or the publishers.

The paper used to print this book comes from sustainable resources.

# Contents

Order No:

Class: ST-9 SOL

Accession No: 114209

Type: 3 week.

Any words appearing in the text in bold, **like this**, are explained in the Glossary.

Many of the photos in this book were taken using a microscope. In the captions you may see a number that tells you how much they have been enlarged. For example, a photo marked '(x200)' is about 200 times bigger than in real life.

# Take a closer look

Modern kitchens are bright, clean places. Surfaces are regularly wiped down, we keep foods that might go off in the fridge, and we cook food to make it safe to eat. It would hard for living creatures to survive. But look closely enough, and you will find plenty of hidden life.

This kitchen may look empty, but up close there is hidden life everywhere.

The magnified view (x2260) of a kitchen scrubbing pad shows thousands of bacteria (tiny ovals) on the pad fibres.

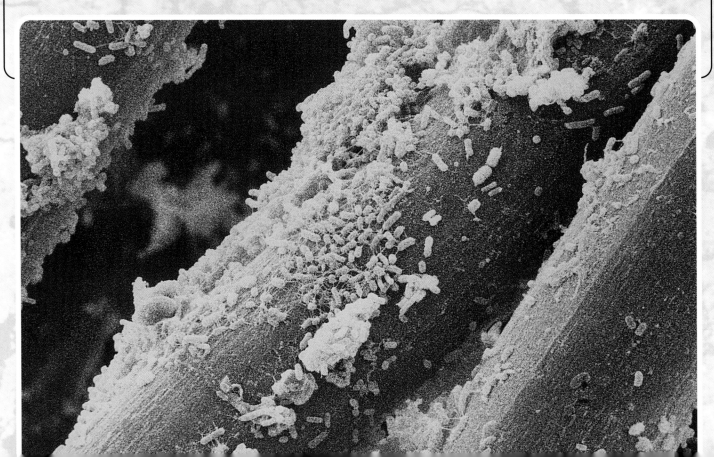

All life, no matter how tiny, needs water and food to survive. Kitchens have plenty of both these things. It's surprising just how many living things manage to find food in even the cleanest and shiniest of kitchens.

## MICROSCOPES

The reason we know about the many kinds of hidden life is because scientists have studied them using microscopes. The kind of microscope that you might have used at school or at home is a light microscope. A powerful one can magnify things up to 1800 times. But to get a close look at really tiny things such as bacteria, you need an **electron microscope**. This can magnify objects up to half a million times.

## Getting up close

Larger insects are occasional visitors to any kitchen. But in most kitchens there are some much smaller insects and minibeasts that we never notice. Most of them live off the crumbs of food that get overlooked, but some can live on dust!

## Closer still

If you looked around your kitchen with a microscope, you would start to find all kinds of **microbes**. Most of these creatures are made of just a single living **cell**. The smallest and most widespread of these single-celled microbes are **bacteria**. But there are also other kinds, such as **fungi** – relatives of the mushrooms you may have had for breakfast.

## Eating microbes

We tend to think of microbes as harmful germs, but some microbes are essential for making our food and drink. We use fungi to make bread, beer and wine, and bacteria to make cheese and yoghurt.

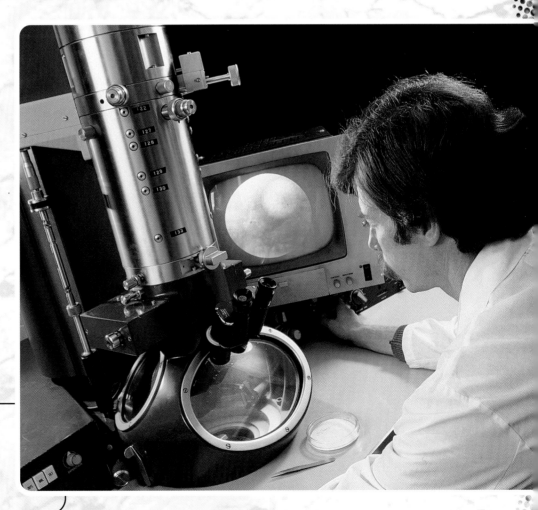

*Electron microscopes are expensive and complicated machines that are used mostly by scientists.*

# Dust-eaters

You might not think that your kitchen is dusty. But on a sunny day, you can see bright specks of dust in the sunlight that streams in through the kitchen window. Normally you don't see this dust, but it's always there – and so are the creatures that live off it.

*Household dust in close-up. This sample contains bits of skin, hairs and clothing fibres, among other things.*

*On a sunny day you can sometimes see dust particles glittering in the light.*

Look closely and you will find that dust is made up of all kinds of things. There are bits of fluff from clothing. There are hairs and pieces of dead insects. There are crumbs of food, cigarette ash, wood shavings, **pollen** and perhaps soil. But one of the main things in household dust is bits of your skin.

## Skin-eating mites

Our skin is always renewing itself, and as new skin is formed the old skin flakes off. These skin flakes are the favourite food of creatures called dust mites.

Mites, including dust mites, are relatives of spiders. This means they have eight legs rather than six. Dust mites live in carpets, furnishings, cracks and dusty corners. They eat mainly human skin, but also any other food that they find.

On average, dust mites live about a month. They take about a month to grow from eggs to adults, going through four different

stages in the process. A female dust mite lays 40 to 100 eggs in her lifetime.

## Dust mite problems

Dust mites themselves are completely harmless to humans. But dust mite droppings, and the skins they cast when they **moult**, become part of the dust in the house, and for some

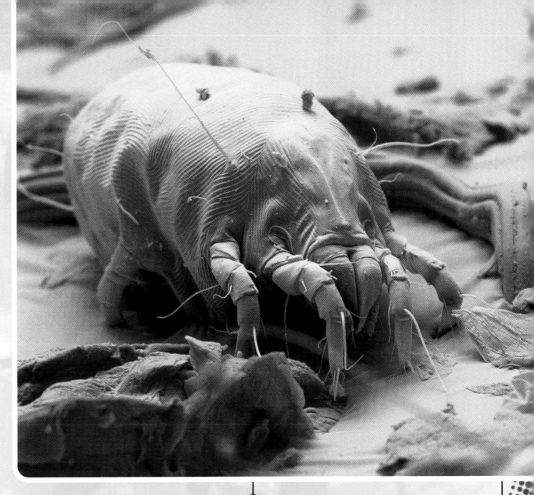

*A dust mite feeding on flakes of skin (x637). Dust mites have no eyes – they find their way around by touch and smell.*

people this can be a problem. Chemicals in them can cause **allergies** in sensitive people. The allergy may be nothing worse than a few sneezes, but some people may get **asthma**.

### NO NEED TO DRINK

Dust mites never need to drink. The air around us contains a certain amount of **water vapour**, and dust mites can absorb some of this water vapour as they breathe. But if the air gets too dry, the mites cannot get enough water vapour, and soon die out.

# Mite pests

Dust mites aren't the only mites you might find in the kitchen. Other kinds of mite are pests too, because they prefer the food we eat to dust and skin.

Some mites are pests of food crops, and several kinds are also pests of household food. Two of these mitey pests are flour mites and cheese mites.

As with dust mites, flour mites go through four different stages before becoming adults. If food is scarce or if the air is dry, young flour mites may go into a **dormant** resting state. When they are resting, the outside of their bodies harden, and the mites hardly move. Mites in this resting stage can survive **pesticides** that would kill a normal mite, and they can live without food or water for up to several months!

## Flour mites

Flour mites feed on all kinds of food, but prefer flour. Flour is most likely to get **infested** with mites if large amounts are kept in warm, slightly damp conditions. A single female mite can lay up to 800 eggs, and it takes only about 10 days for the eggs to become adults, so one mite can quickly become a serious infestation. Flour infested with mites has a sharp smell and causes an upset stomach if eaten.

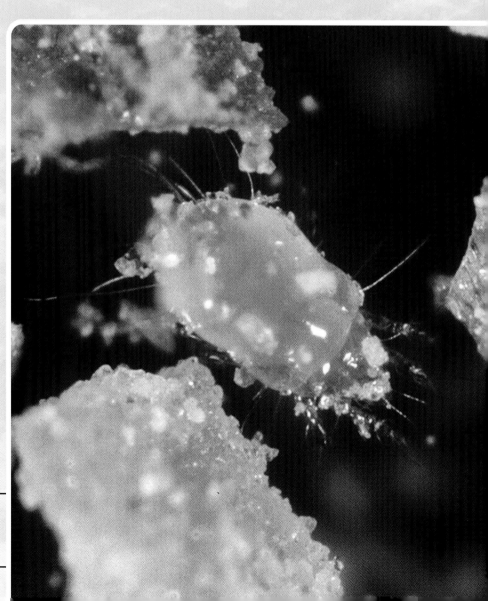

A flour mite feeding on pieces of bran flour.

## Cheese mites

Cheese mites are also sometimes found in flour, but they prefer cheese. As with flour mites, cheese mites prefer warm, damp conditions, so cheese kept in the fridge is unlikely to become infested. If a cheese does get infested with mites, it becomes covered in a grey powder, which is a mixture of mites, mite droppings and their shed skins.

Most cheeses are spoiled if they become infested with mites. However, in the Altenberg region of Germany the makers of one type of cheese deliberately add cheese mites to the newly made cheese, and then leave it to ripen. When the cheese is covered with a grey powdery coating, it is ready to eat. Not surprisingly, this kind of cheese is not to everyone's taste!

### TINY HITCH-HIKERS

To move out of a place where conditions are not good, mites often hitch a lift on a larger creature. Many kinds of mite move from place to place by clinging on to the legs or other parts of a large insect.

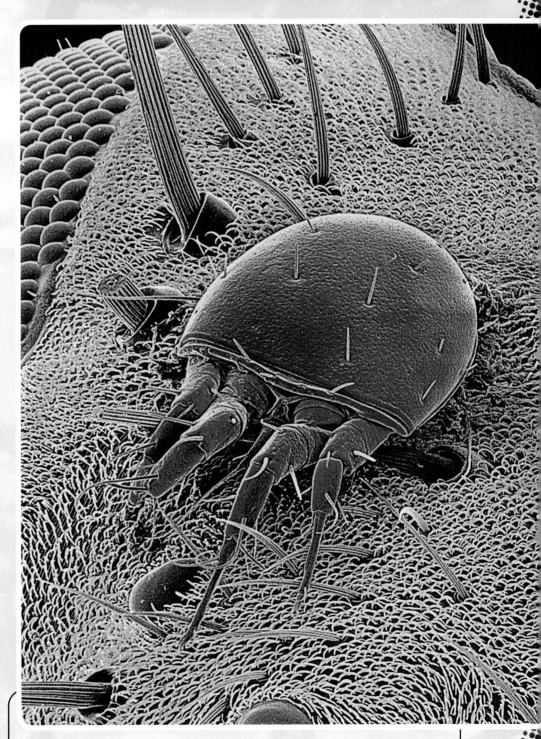

A mite hitching a ride on the head of a fly (you can see the fly's eye, top left). Usually this hitch-hiking does not affect the insect carrier, but large numbers of mites can weigh it down or even kill it.

# Yeasts in the bread

If you have ever made bread, you will know that you use **yeast** to make the bread rise. Yeast is a tiny living thing – a type of **fungus**. Most people use dried yeast to make bread. Yeast can survive being dried out because it goes into a resting state, rather like flour mites do. If you add warm water and sugar, the yeast becomes active again.

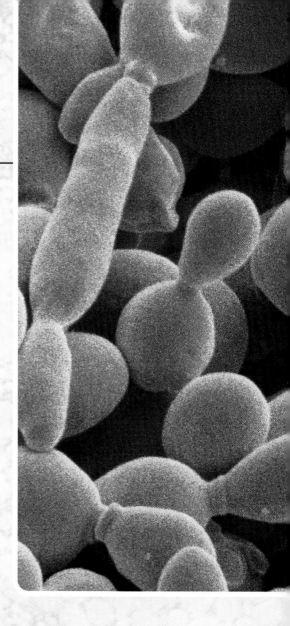

Bread rises because of the carbon dioxide produced by tiny yeast cells in the bread dough.

## Yeasts in bread

Yeast is a very tiny creature made of just a single **cell**. If you keep yeast cells warm and give them sugary food, they will grow and reproduce. They break down the sugar to get energy. A waste product of this process is **carbon dioxide** gas.

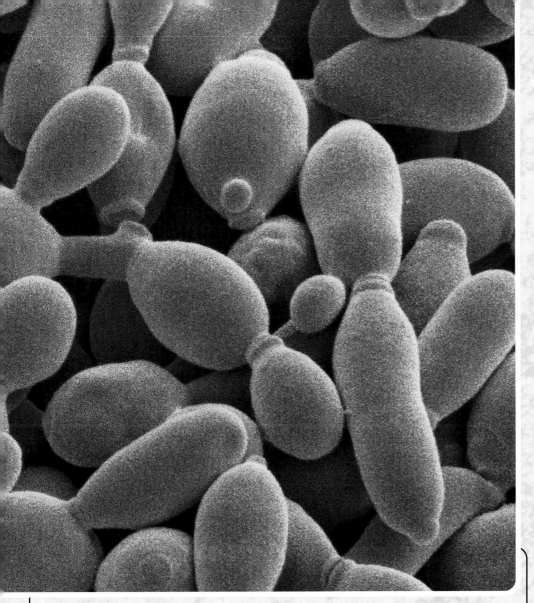

## Yeasts in beer

As well as producing carbon dioxide, yeast cells produce alcohol when they break down sugars. So yeast is also used to make beers and wines. The yeast is **fermented** (see the box) with a sugary liquid and it produces alcohol. In beer-making the sugary liquid is usually made from barley, while in wine-making the liquid is grape juice.

The type of yeast used for bread-making produces lots of carbon dioxide but not much alcohol, while beer-making yeast does the opposite.

*A magnified view (x8277) of the kind of yeast used in brewing and baking. Yeast cells reproduce by 'budding' off new cells. Some budding cells can be seen in this photo.*

Bread dough is basically flour and water mixed up to make a thick dough. If you add yeast to this mixture, it uses the **starch** in the flour as food and begins to produce carbon dioxide. Bubbles of gas get trapped in the dough, making it light and airy. When you put the bread in the oven, the yeast cells continue to grow and produce carbon dioxide for a short time. But eventually the bread becomes too hot, and the yeast is killed.

## LIFE WITHOUT AIR

Most living things need **oxygen** to help them get energy from their food. This is why they have to breathe. But yeasts and some other **microbes** can get energy from their food without using oxygen. This process is known as fermentation. Alcohol and carbon dioxide are the waste products.

# Microbes in other foods

Have you ever opened a bottle of milk, sniffed it and realized that the milk is off? Milk goes off because **bacteria** grow in it and make it sour. But we get those bacteria to work for us when making cheese and yoghurt.

Cheese and yoghurt are both made by **fermenting** milk in different ways. The process is similar to that used for bread-making, except that bacteria are used rather than yeast. Bacteria are added to milk, and they use sugars in the milk as food. Waste products that the bacteria produce as they grow change the milk in useful ways.

Lactobacillus bulgaricus (*orange, rod-shaped, top left*) and Streptococcus thermophilis (*orange, spherical in chains*) can be used to make yoghurt and cheese.

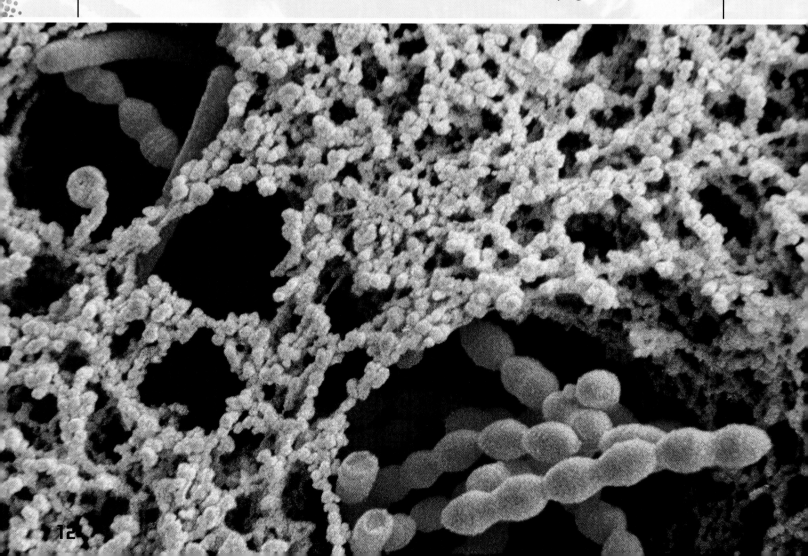

In some cheeses, a mould **fungus** is added as well as the bacteria. In blue cheese the mould gives the cheese its blue 'veins'.

## Yoghurt-making

To make yoghurt, milk is left to ferment with a particular type of bacteria. The waste product that the bacteria produces is an **acid** (lactic acid). The acid is what gives yoghurt its sharp taste. This is similar to what happens when milk goes off, but in sour milk there are also many other kinds of bacteria, and some of them produce unpleasant tastes.

## Cheese-making

Cheese-making uses the same kind of bacteria as for yoghurt-making. As with yoghurt, the bacteria produce acid, which **curdles** the milk and gives it a sharp taste. But a substance called **rennet** is also added to the milk, which makes it separate into a white solid (curds) and a thin, watery liquid (whey).

In the next stage, the whey is drained off, and the curds are cut up and salted. The salt slows the fermentation reaction, so that the cheese does not become too sharp-tasting.

The curds are squeezed in a press to remove more liquid. Then the cheese is left to ripen for a few weeks or months. During ripening, the bacteria in the cheese continue to grow slowly, and help give the cheese flavour.

*Cheeses ripening in a cool store. Ripe cheese still has living bacteria in it, but they are killed by the acid in our stomach when we eat the cheese.*

# Mouldy food

We say that when food goes off it is mouldy. This is because it is often **moulds** that spoil food. Moulds are **fungi**, related to mushrooms and to the yeasts used for making bread and beer.

*The green mould on this orange is caused by a mould called Penicillium. One type of Penicillium is important medically, because the **antibiotic** penicillin is made from it. Penicillium uses the antibiotic as a chemical weapon to get rid of bacteria that compete with it for food.*

## Going mouldy

So what happens when, for instance, an orange goes mouldy? The mould begins as a small white spot, which then spreads. Once the spot gets to a certain size, it begins to turn green at the centre, and the green area quickly grows. After four or five days the whole orange may be covered in green mould.

Like other fungi, moulds are made up of tiny threads, or **hyphae**, and they reproduce by releasing **spores** (see box). The white spot at the start of the infection is formed by a tangle of growing hyphae. The white mould then turns green as spores begin to form on tiny stalks above the body of the fungus.

## Doing an important job

Moulds are a nuisance because they can spoil our food, but they also do an important job. They are

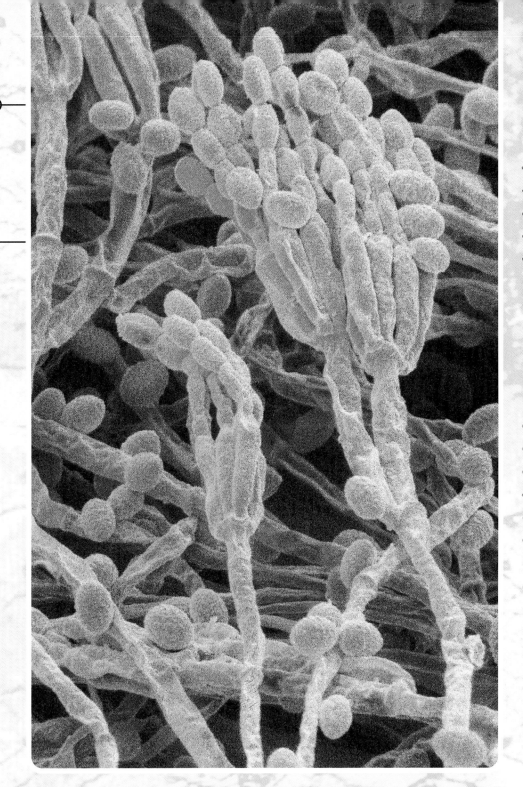

*A magnified photo (x2855) showing the spore-producing structures of Penicillium. The round shapes on the ends of the hyphae are spores.*

part of nature's recycling system, which breaks down the bodies of dead animals and plants and releases their **nutrients** back into the environment.

Obviously, we don't want moulds to recycle the fruit and bread that we wish to eat. But moulds also break down tough materials such as wood, and unpleasant ones such as animal droppings. Only moulds and other fungi can digest some of the chemicals in wood and turn them into useful nutrients.

## FUNGAL FACTS

Fungi are neither plants nor animals. They do not make their own food as plants do and they don't 'eat' food like animals. Instead they grow into their food and absorb nutrients from it. Most fungi either grow on dead or rotting material, or they are **parasites**.

Fungi usually grow as microscopic threads called hyphae. The body of the fungus is a tangle of these threads. They reproduce by making millions of tiny 'seeds' called spores.

When foods go off, **moulds** are not the only culprits. They get a lot of help from **bacteria**. There are always small numbers of bacteria on food, but once they begin to grow and reproduce, they make food taste bad.

There are bacteria around us all the time. They live on your skin, on your pets and on other animals and plants. There are bacteria floating in the air, and on most of the surfaces in the house.

There are bacteria on fresh food, and if conditions are right (see box), they will multiply. A population of about a million bacteria is enough to make food taste 'off'.

*Before it is sold, milk is usually **pasteurized** (heated gently) to get rid of bacteria. Even so, milk goes off very quickly if it is left out of the fridge.*

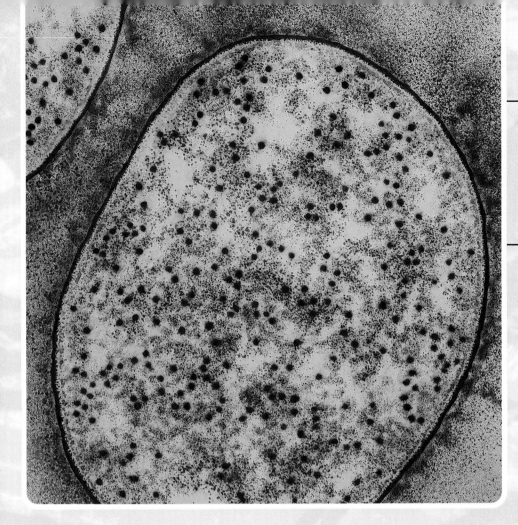

Psychrobacter *bacteria (x108,000) like this one are specialized to grow in cold conditions. They can spoil food even in the fridge.*

This is fine in yoghurt and cheese, but it makes many foods taste sour and unpleasant.

## What conditions cause spoilage?

Many different kinds of bacteria cause spoilage. Which kinds develop on food depends on how the food is kept. For instance, many bacteria grow best at 'normal' temperatures, from about 5 to 20°C, and will do well if food is left out in normal conditions. However, some bacteria grow well at temperatures as low as 0°C, and these can cause food to spoil even in the fridge. Other kinds grow best in hot conditions, and these can spoil food that has been cooked and left in a warm place.

## How do bacteria spoil food?

A bacterium doesn't have a mouth to eat its food with. Instead, it releases chemicals called **enzymes** into the food. The enzymes break the food down into **nutrients** that the bacterium can absorb. One of the things that happens when food spoils is that it goes mushy or liquid, and this is caused by bacterial enzymes.

Like people and other animals, bacteria produce wastes. These are often another cause of food spoilage. Some bacteria produce **acid** as waste.

## BREEDING BACTERIA

Large numbers of bacteria can build up on food incredibly quickly. Under ideal conditions, some kinds of bacteria can reproduce every 20 minutes. At this speed, a single bacterium could produce several million others within 8 hours.

# Stopping spoilage

People have developed many different ways of making food keep longer without spoiling. Most of these methods are based on understanding how **microbes** spread and grow.

### Cooling and drying

Like other living things, most **bacteria** grow best in warm conditions, although as we saw on page 17, some bacteria like the cold. They also need water in order to grow and multiply.

One way we can stop foods from spoiling is to keep them in the fridge or freezer. The low temperatures kill many kinds of bacteria, and even those that survive cannot grow quickly.

Since bacteria need water, another way to stop food spoiling is to keep it dry. Fresh food naturally contains lots of water, so to really make this work you have to dry the food. For thousands of years people have been preserving food by drying it. More recently we have developed new dried foods such as powdered soup and pasta.

*Food can be made to last longer by various ways. Pickling, drying, canning and freezing are a few of them.*

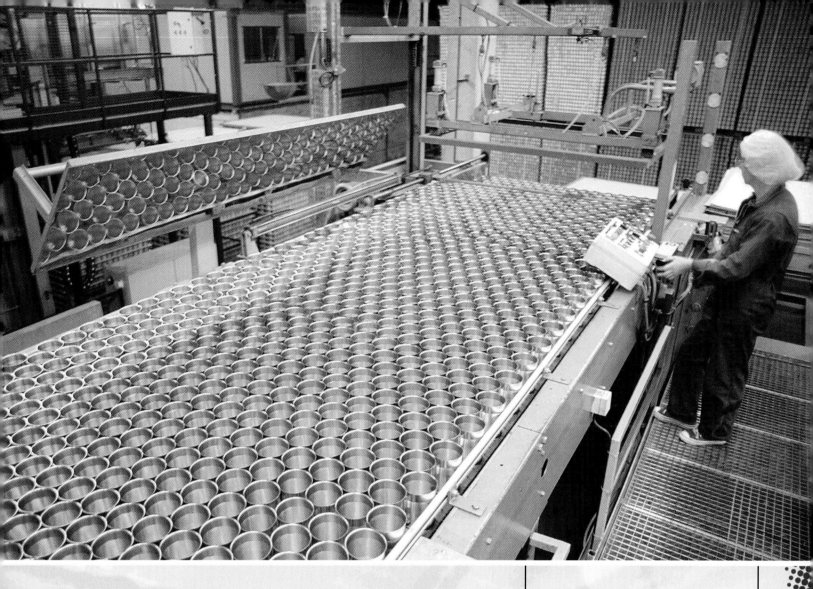

## Pickling and salting

Most kinds of bacteria do not like **acid** conditions – this is one of the reasons that cheese keeps longer than milk. Pickling foods in vinegar makes them very acidic, and they keep longer. You can pickle all kinds of foods, from eggs or herrings to apricots.

Another way of stopping bacteria growing is to add salt to food. The most obvious salted foods are nuts and crisps. Butter is often salted, and some kinds of meat and fish.

## Canning and irradiation

When food is canned it is heated to get rid of the bacteria, and then put in sealed cans, so that no new bacteria can get in. Many kinds of canned food will keep for years without spoiling.

A more recent way of getting rid of bacteria on food is irradiation. This involves bombarding food with gamma rays (a type of radiation similar to X-rays). Irradiation kills virtually all bacteria on food, so it will keep much longer. But many people are unhappy with the idea of eating irradiated food, and some think it is harmful.

*A cannery plant is a very clean and sterile place where no bacteria can grow.*

# Food-poisoning bacteria

You have soup for dinner, and your parents forget to put the leftovers in the fridge. The next day, you heat up the remains of the soup for lunch. Two days later you feel awful: you are sick and have a high temperature. The soup was full of food-poisoning **bacteria**.

Cooking kills most bacteria, but if you leave soup out overnight a few bacteria might get into it. In warm, wet soup, bacteria can multiply very quickly. Even large numbers of some kinds of bacteria will do no harm, but other kinds can make you ill.

## Bacterial poisons

Different bacteria cause food poisoning in different ways. Some kinds produce toxins (poisons) as they grow in the food, and these make you ill.

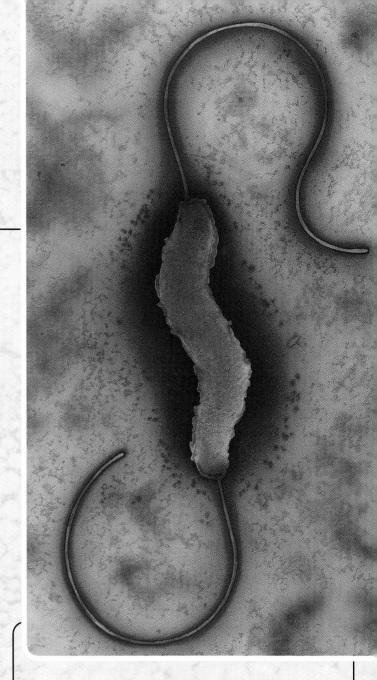

Campylobacter *(x33,530) is another common cause of food poisoning. It is an unusual bacterium because of its spiral shape. It has long, whip-like 'tails' at either end that enable it to move quickly.*

*Staphylococcus aureus* is a bacterium that can cause food poisoning in this way. It is most often found in cooked meat or chicken. Large numbers of the bacteria need to grow before infected food will make you ill, but if so, then heating will not get rid of the toxin.

## Tough survivors

Other bacteria only need to be present in small numbers on the food, because they survive in your gut (digestive tract) and multiply there. They cause damage to your gut lining, and this is what makes you ill. This kind of food poisoning shows its symptoms later, because it takes a few days for the bacteria to multiply in the gut.

The bacteria *Salmonella* and *Escherichia coli* cause food poisoning in this way. *Salmonella* is found in many kinds of food, but especially in raw meat and eggs. *E. coli* exist in several different types or strains. Some of these normally live in the lower part of our gut without causing ill effects. However, others, found in raw meat, **unpasteurized** milk and **contaminated** water, can cause serious food poisoning.

## Avoiding food poisoning

If you are careful about how you prepare your food, you are unlikely to get food poisoning. Wash raw food well before you eat it, and check that meat and chicken are properly cooked before you eat them. And make sure you don't leave soup (or any other cooked food) out overnight!

Clostridium botulinum *is a very rare cause of food poisoning, but it can be deadly. It produces an extremely powerful toxin, one of the most poisonous substances known.*

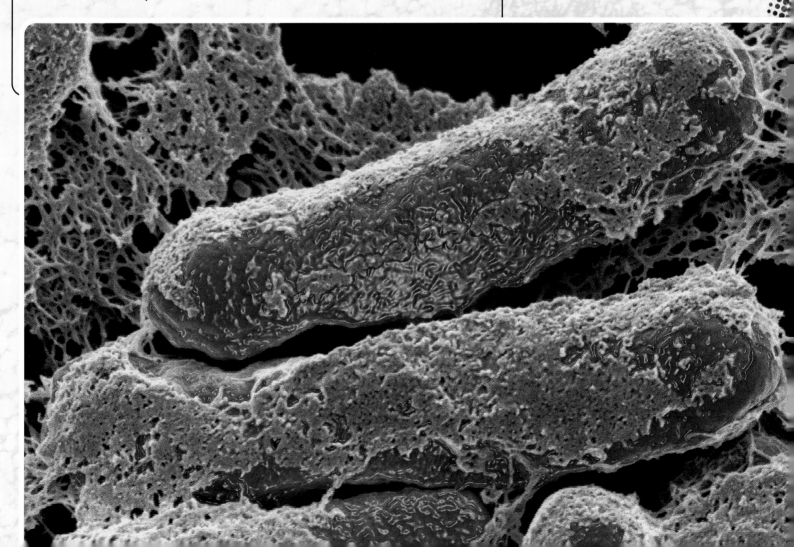

# Surface microbes

No matter how clean a kitchen looks, there will be **microbes** everywhere. In most places there are only a few, and without food and water they will not multiply. But in some parts of the kitchen, **bacteria** grow in large numbers. One place is in the waste bin – another is on chopping boards!

Bacteria are always landing on kitchen surfaces, or being transferred there from your skin. Most of these bacteria do not multiply because there is no food for them. Many microbes dry out and die on these surfaces (although they are soon replaced). However, some bacteria go into a 'resting state' until conditions improve (see box).

*The surface of a chopping board has plenty of grooves and cracks where bacteria and food particles can get stuck.*

*Many people separate out their kitchen scraps to go into the garden compost. A scrap bucket needs a good lid, because it is an ideal breeding ground for bacteria.*

## Microbe hang-outs

Microbes do grow in large numbers in some parts of the kitchen. One obvious bacterial hang-out is the waste bin. Here there is plenty of food for them, and it is often damp. Other places are on kitchen cloths, sponges and tea towels. These places are often damp or wet, and tiny food particles get caught in them.

Chopping boards have many grooves and holes where bacteria can build up. Cracks or chips in crockery or wooden spoons can be microbe traps. And **mould** can grow on damp paint or wallpaper.

## Keeping microbes down

One of the best ways to keep the numbers of microbes down in the kitchen is to wash your hands before preparing food. But make sure you dry them well, because dampness helps microbes to spread. Also, change tea towels, sponges and cloths regularly and wash chopping boards with hot water and detergent.

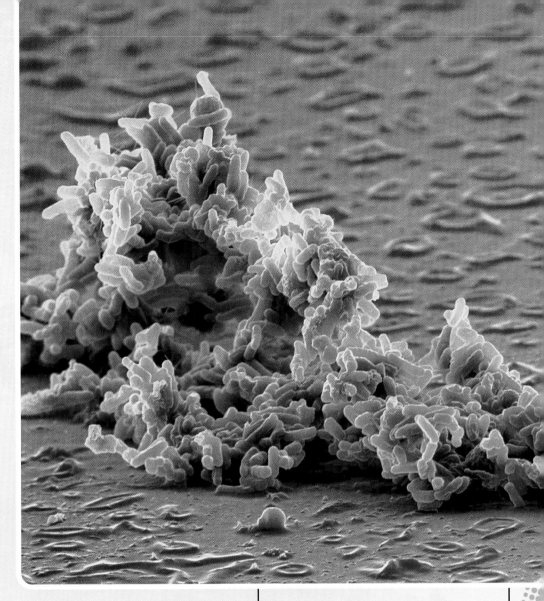

*Bacteria found on kitchen surfaces come from many sources. These Enterobacter cloacae bacteria (x3770) are normally found in the gut.*

## BACTERIAL SPORES

Some bacteria can form thick-coated **spores** when they find themselves in harsh conditions. Inside the spore, the bacterium lies **dormant**. It can survive drying out, low and high temperatures, and harmful chemicals. If conditions improve, a new bacterium grows from the spore. The spores of some bacteria can survive for hundreds of years.

# Microbes in the drains

Have you ever seen someone cleaning out the waste pipe of the kitchen sink? The inside of the pipe is often coated with a layer of smelly slime. This slime is a mega-city for **microbes** known as a **biofilm**.

*Micrograph of a slightly scratched plughole from a kitchen sink. Limescale deposits trap dirt and encourage the growth of bacteria.*

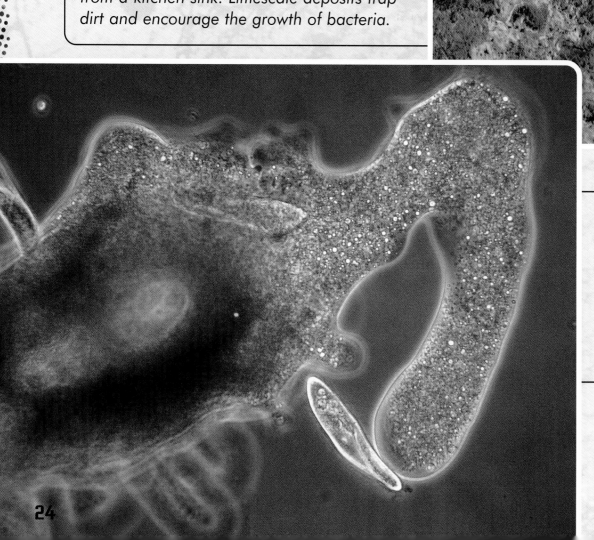

*This amoeba is about to capture another, smaller protozoan (at lower right) using its extended pseudopods (x240).*

Biofilms form quickly on wet surfaces where there is a supply of food. Kitchen drains are ideal places, because waste water from the kitchen sink includes material that microbes can feed on. Biofilms can also form on the hulls of ships, on our teeth – even on contact lenses!

## How biofilms form

Biofilms are first formed by **bacteria**. They attach to the wet surface and begin to grow. As the bacteria multiply, they begin to produce large amounts of sticky slime. They glue themselves together to form tall towers and mushroom shapes. Between the towers are water channels, which allow water and food to reach the bacteria.

As well as cementing them together, the slime protects the bacteria from the surrounding environment. Chemicals such as disinfectant and bleach are much less effective against bacteria protected by this slime coating. Brushing and scrubbing is needed to get rid of them.

## Microbe grazers

Once a sticky sludge begins to grow and thicken, other microbes arrive that 'graze' on the biofilm. Most belong to a group of microbes called **protozoa**.

**Amoebas** are usually the first protozoans to arrive.

They move over a surface by stretching out long, finger-like projections, called **pseudopods**, and anchoring them to the surface, then pulling themselves forward. To feed, they flow around a bacterium or other food, and then engulf it completely.

Other protozoa that arrive later are called **ciliates**. These kinds of protozoa have many tiny 'hairs', called **cilia**, which beat backwards and forwards. They use these to swim about and to capture food.

*A ciliate (green) and bacteria (red and blue) in a compost heap (x1785). Ciliates often use their cilia to move food, including bacteria, into their mouths.*

# Wheel animals

**Bacteria** and single-**celled** creatures are not the only **microbes** in drain slime; there are tiny animals too. Rotifers are a group of animals with a 'wheel' of **cilia** around their mouth.

Rotifers are not just found in drains. There are over 2000 kinds of rotifers, living just about anywhere there is fresh water. In Antarctic lakes there are such large numbers that they turn the water red. But they can also live in a drain or a patch of damp mud.

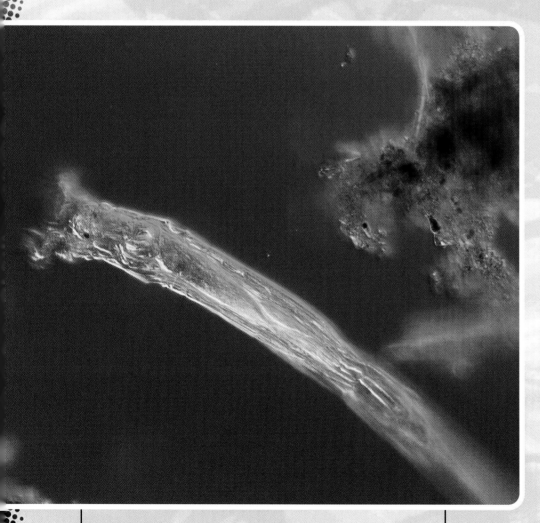

**Rotifers**
Although they are as small as many **protozoans**, rotifers are actually multi-celled animals. They have one or more light-sensing organs, muscles and a simple gut. Many kinds have soft, transparent bodies, but some are encased in a shell.

Rotifers get their name from the one or two rings of cilia that surround their mouth. The cilia beat in rapid waves, which make it look as if the whole ring is rotating like a wheel. The beating cilia draw currents of water into their mouth.

*Rotifers use strong muscles to suck prey into their stomachs (x250).*

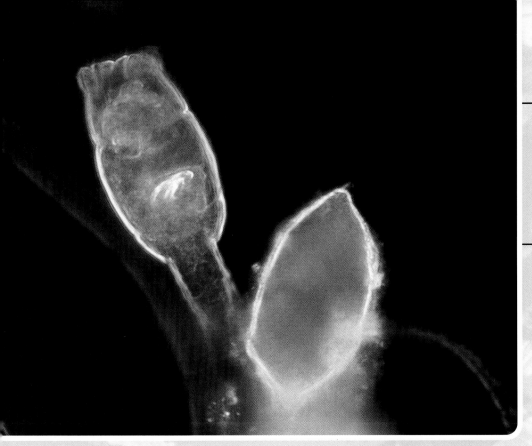

Rotifers reproduce by forming eggs. This photo (x538) shows a rotifier (left) hatching from an egg case (right).

themselves. In this state they can survive a baking hot sun or freezing cold winds. They are small enough to be blown in air currents, and when they land in a wetter location they come out of their protective casing.

Rotifers can swim freely, like Keratella, or they can attach themselves to something with their sticky foot. The kinds of rotifers in drains tend to be ones that stay attached rather than swimming freely.

One of the reasons that rotifers are so successful is that they can survive long periods out of water. If the water they are in dries up, they form a protective envelope around

Conochilus *rotifers form colonies by joining together in a ball. They attach to each other via their sticky foot.*

Many rotifers are filter-feeders, sifting particles of food from the currents of water drawn into their mouth. Others are **predators**, using strong muscles to suck microbes into their stomach. Food goes first to a part of the gut called the mastax, which has a set of hard 'jaws' to grind the food up.

# Table of sizes

Although all hidden life is tiny, there is a huge range of sizes. To a flea, a grain of pollen seems just as tiny as the flea seems to us!

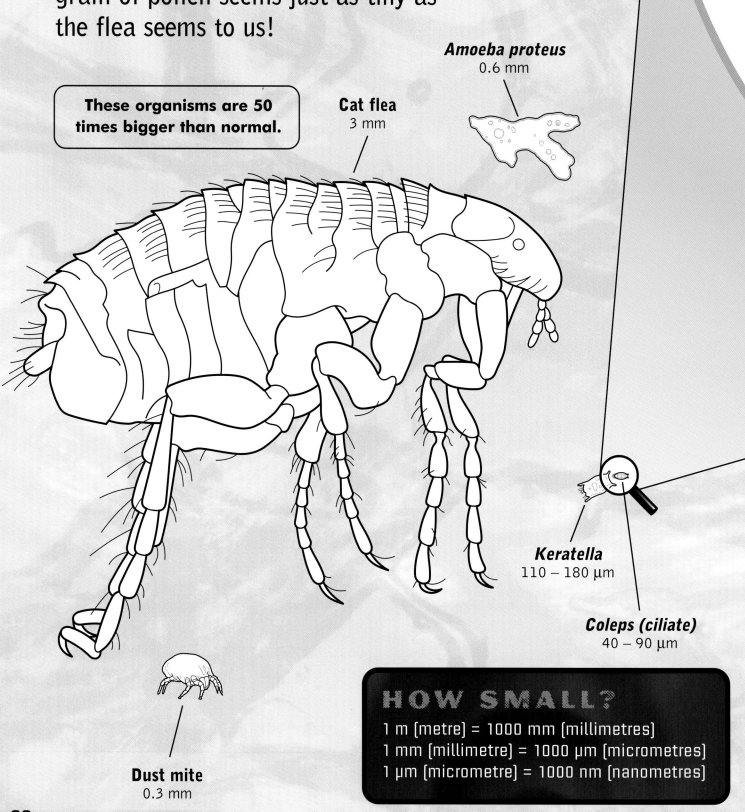

**These organisms are 50 times bigger than normal.**

**Cat flea**
3 mm

*Amoeba proteus*
0.6 mm

*Keratella*
110 – 180 μm

*Coleps (ciliate)*
40 – 90 μm

**Dust mite**
0.3 mm

### HOW SMALL?

1 m (metre) = 1000 mm (millimetres)
1 mm (millimetre) = 1000 μm (micrometres)
1 μm (micrometre) = 1000 nm (nanometres)

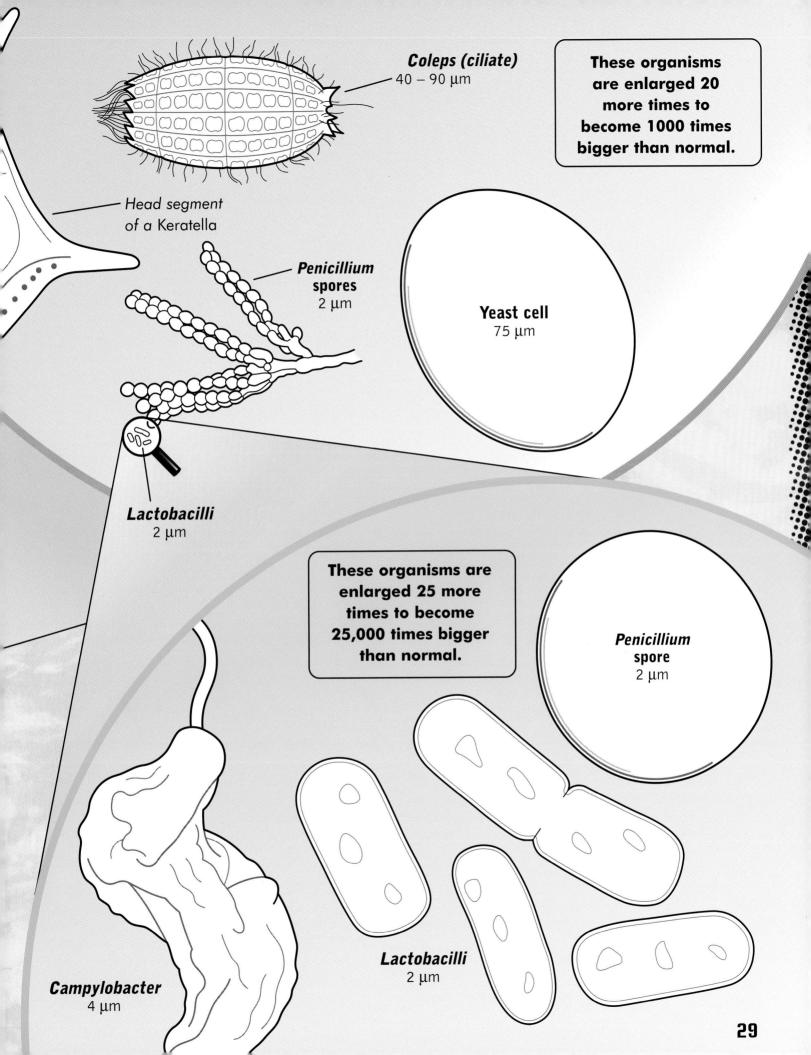

Coleps (ciliate)
40 – 90 μm

These organisms are enlarged 20 more times to become 1000 times bigger than normal.

Head segment of a Keratella

*Penicillium* spores
2 μm

Yeast cell
75 μm

*Lactobacilli*
2 μm

These organisms are enlarged 25 more times to become 25,000 times bigger than normal.

*Penicillium* spore
2 μm

*Campylobacter*
4 μm

*Lactobacilli*
2 μm

# Glossary

**acid**   a sour, sharp or corrosive substance. Vinegar and lemon juice are acidic.

**allergy**   when the body overreacts to something that you breathe in or eat or get on your skin. It can cause sneezing, or a rash, or a sickness such as asthma.

**amoebas**   single-celled microbes that move and catch food by sending out finger-like projections

**antibiotics**   drugs that kill bacteria or stop them growing

**asthma**   disease of the lungs that causes wheezing and other breathing difficulties

**bacteria**   (singular – bacterium) very tiny creatures, each one only a single cell. They are different from other single-celled creatures because they do not have a nucleus.

**biofilm**   sticky, smelly layer of microbes and slime

**carbon dioxide**   gas that is found in small amounts in the air. There is also some carbon dioxide dissolved in water.

**cells**   building blocks of living things. Some living things are single just cells, others are made up of billions of cells working together.

**cilia**   (singular – cilium) tiny 'hairs' that stick out from the surface of some microbes. They can move in a co-ordinated way to propel the microbe along or waft food towards it.

**ciliates**   group of microbes that have cilia

**contaminate**   to become dirty or infected with disease microbes

**curdle**   when milk curdles it separates into a solid (curds) and a thin liquid (whey)

**dormant**   lying inactive, as if in a deep sleep

**electron microscopes**   very powerful microscopes that can magnify objects up to half a million times

**enzymes**   chemicals that are used by living cells to do such things as break down food into simple nutrients

**ferment**   when food ferments, tiny microbes turn the sugar in the food into another substance, such as an acid or alcohol

**fungi**   (singular – fungus) plant-like living things such as mushrooms and yeasts

**hyphae**   thin, thread-like cells that make up the body of most fungi

**infestation**   when something is overrun with a harmful or irritating creature such as an insect

**larvae**   (singular – larva) young stage of some types of creatures. Larvae look different from adults, and may have to go through a changing stage in order to become adults.

**microbes**   microscopic creatures such as bacteria, protozoa, fungi and viruses

**mould**   a type of fungus that can grow on or in a wide range of substances, from damp plaster to cheese

**moult**   to shed hair, feathers or skin. When an insect moults it sheds its hard outer skeleton in order to grow. Under the old skeleton is a new one, which is soft at first and so can be expanded to a bigger size.

**nutrients**   chemicals that nourish living things

**oxygen**   gas that is found in the air and dissolved in water. Most living things need oxygen to live.

**parasites**   creatures that live on or in another living creature and take their food from it, without giving any benefit in return

**pasteurization**   process of purification, usually for milk, in which it is heated to a specific temperature for a specific period of time in order to kill harmful microbes

**pesticides**   chemicals that are used to kill insects or other animals that are pests, for instance those that eat crops or cause disease

**pollen**   fine powder produced by flowers. If pollen is carried by the wind or insects to other flowers of the same kind, it fertilizes them.

**predator**   animal that hunts and kills another animal for food.

**protozoa**   single-celled creatures that have larger, more complicated cells than bacteria

**pseudopods**   finger-like projections that amoebas send out in order to move around and to capture food

**rennet**   material made from the stomachs of young calves that is used to curdle milk in cheese-making

**spores**   fungal spores are like very tiny fungal 'seeds'. Bacterial spores are bacteria that have formed a tough outer coat to help them survive difficult conditions.

**starch**   the main substance in flour. Starch can be broken down by enzymes into sugars.

**unpasteurized**   when a product has not been through the pasteurization process

**water vapour**   water as a gas. The air around us contains some water vapour.

**yeast**   microscopic, single-celled type of fungus

# further reading

*Bugs & Minibeasts (The Illustrated Wildlife Encyclopedia)*, John Farndon, Jen Green and Barbara Taylor, (Southwater Press, 2002)

*Cells and Life: The Diversity of Life*, Robert Snedden, (Heinemann Library, 2002)

*Cells and Life: The World of the Cell*, Robert Snedden, (Heinemann Library, 2002)

*DK Mega Bites: Microlife: The Microscopic World of Tiny Creatures*, David Burnie, (Dorling Kindersley, 2002)

*Horrible Science: Microscopic Monsters*, Nick Arnold, (illustrated by Tony de Saulles) (Barbour Books, 2001)

*Microlife: A World of Microorganisms*, Robert Snedden, (Heinemann Library, 2000)

*Spiders and Scorpions (Awesome Bugs)*, Anna Claybourne, (Franklin Watts, 2003)

# Websites

**Cells Alive! (www.cellsalive.com)**
Pictures, videos and interactive pages about cells and microbes. The How Big? page shows the sizes of creatures from mites to viruses.

**Virtual Microscopy (www.micro.magnet.fsu.edu/primer/virtual/virtual.html)**
On this interactive website you can pick from a selection of samples, adjust the focus, change the magnification, and use a whole range of powerful microscopes.

**Microbe Zoo (www.commtechlab.msu.edu/sites/dlc-me/zoo/zoutline.htm)**
A site about strange creatures from the world of microbes. Includes information about biofilms in the 'Animal Pavilion' section.

**The Smallest Page on the Web (www.microscopy-uk.org.uk/mag/wimsmall/smal1.html)**
This site shows some of the microbes you can find in a freshwater pond. It includes photos and information on amoebas, ciliates and rotifers.

# Index